FOR:_____

*W*ithout faith it is impossible to please God.
Hebrews 11:6

FROM: _____

Words of Faith
Copyright 1998 by the Zondervan Corporation
ISBN 0-310-97735-5

Requests for information should be addressed to:  ZondervanPublishingHouse
Mail Drop B20
Grand Rapids, Michigan 49530
http://www.zondervan.com

Senior Editor: Gwen Ellis
Project Editor: Sarah M. Hupp
Art Director: Patti Matthews

Printed in China
99 00 01 02 / HK / 5 4 3

WORDS

OF FAITH

FOR A WOMAN OF FAITH

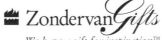
Zondervan*Gifts*

We have a gift for inspiration™

WORDS OF FAITH

What Is Faith?

I am not ashamed of the gospel, because it is the power of God for the salvation of everyone who believes: first for the Jew, then for the Gentile. For in the gospel a righteousness from God is revealed, a righteousness that is by faith from first to last, just as it is written: "The righteous will live by faith."

Romans 1:16–17

Those who trust in the LORD are like Mount Zion, which cannot be shaken but endures forever.

Psalm 125:1

$\mathcal{T}$rust in the LORD with all your heart and lean not
on your own understanding; in all your ways
acknowledge him, and he will
make your paths straight.

Proverbs 3:5–6

$\mathcal{I}$f you believe, you will receive whatever
you ask for in prayer.

Matthew 21:22

$\mathcal{T}$he LORD delights in those who fear him, who put
their hope in his unfailing love.

Psalm 147:11

I sought the LORD, and he answered me; he delivered me from all my fears. Those who look to him are radiant; their faces are never covered with shame. The angel of the LORD encamps around those who fear him, and he delivers them. Taste and see that the LORD is good.

Psalm 34:4–5,7–8

Command those who are rich in this present world not to be arrogant nor to put their hope in wealth, which is so uncertain, but to put their hope in God.

1 Timothy 6:17

$\mathcal{J}$esus said: "I am the resurrection and the life. He who believes in me will live, even though he dies; and whoever lives and believes in me will never die."

John 11:25–26

$\mathcal{P}$ursue righteousness, godliness, faith, love, endurance and gentleness. Fight the good fight of the faith. Take hold of the eternal life to which you were called.

1 Timothy 6:11–12

Everyone born of God overcomes the world. This is the victory that has overcome the world, even our faith.

1 John 5:4

For it is by grace you have been saved, through faith—and this not from yourselves, it is the gift of God.

Ephesians 2:8

Since we have been justified through faith, we have peace with God through our Lord Jesus Christ.

Romans 5:1

*W*e fix our eyes not on what is seen, but on what is unseen. For what is seen is temporary, but what is unseen is eternal.

2 Corinthians 4:18

*T*hese are written that you may believe that Jesus is the Christ, the Son of God, and that by believing you may have life in his name.

John 20:31

*T*he righteous will live by his faith.

Habakkuk 2:4

$\mathcal{N}$ow for a little while you may have had to suffer grief in all kinds of trials. These have come so that your faith—of greater worth than gold, which perishes even though refined by fire—may be proved genuine and may result in praise, glory and honor when Jesus Christ is revealed. Though you have not seen him, you love him; and even though you do not see him now, you believe in him and are filled with an inexpressible and glorious joy, for you are receiving the goal of your faith, the salvation of your souls.

1 Peter 1:6–9

$\mathcal{F}$or it is with your heart that you believe and are justified.

Romans 10:10

To all who received him, to those who believed in his name, he gave the right to become children of God.

John 1:12

Whoever believes in the Son has eternal life, but whoever rejects the Son will not see life.

John 3:36

My Father's will is that everyone who looks to the Son and believes in him shall have eternal life, and I will raise him up at the last day.

John 6:40

$\mathcal{D}$o not conform any longer to the pattern of this world, but be transformed by the renewing of your mind. Then you will be able to test and approve what God's will is—his good, pleasing and perfect will.

Romans 12:2

$\mathcal{A}$nyone who believes in the Son of God has this testimony in his heart. Anyone who does not believe God has made him out to be a liar, because he has not believed the testimony God has given about his Son. And this is the testimony: God has given us eternal life, and this life is in his Son.

1 John 5:10–11

WHY FAITH IS
IMPORTANT

*W*ithout faith it is impossible to please God, because anyone who comes to him must believe that he exists and that he rewards those who earnestly seek him.

Hebrews 11:6

*F*or in Christ Jesus neither circumcision nor uncircumcision has any value. The only thing that counts is faith expressing itself through love.

Galatians 5:6

*W*hoever believes in me, as the Scripture has said, streams of living water will flow from within him.

John 7:38

*S*ince the promise of entering his rest still stands, let us be careful that none of you be found to have fallen short of it. For we also have had the gospel preached to us, just as they did; but the message they heard was of no value to them, because those who heard did not combine it with faith.

Hebrews 4:1–2

*W*hoever believes in him is not condemned, but whoever does not believe stands condemned already because he has not believed in the name of God's one and only Son.

John 3:18

*A*cknowledge the God of your father, and serve him with wholehearted devotion and with a willing mind, for the LORD searches every heart and understands every motive behind the thoughts. If you seek him, he will be found by you.

1 Chronicles 28:9

"You will seek me and find me when you seek me with all your heart. I will be found by you," declares the LORD.

Jeremiah 29:13–14

*B*e all the more eager to make your calling and election sure. For if you do these things, you will never fall.

2 Peter 1:10

The LORD said to Moses and Aaron, "Because you did not trust in me enough to honor me as holy in the sight of the Israelites, you will not bring this community into the land I give them."

Numbers 20:12

Faith by itself, if it is not accompanied by action, is dead. But someone will say, "You have faith; I have deeds." Show me your faith without deeds, and I will show you my faith by what I do.

James 2:17–18

We work with you for your joy, because it is by faith you stand firm.

2 Corinthians 1:24

$\mathcal{E}$verything that does not come from faith is sin.

Romans 14:23

$\mathcal{H}$ave faith in the Lᵃᵃᵃ your God and you will be
upheld; have faith in his prophets and
you will be successful.

2 Chronicles 20:20

$\mathcal{T}$hey were broken off because of unbelief,
and you stand by faith.

Romans 11:20

$\mathcal{B}$elieve in the Lord Jesus, and you will be saved—
you and your household.

Acts 16:31

$\mathcal{K}$now that a man is not justified by observing the law, but by faith in Jesus Christ. So we, too, have put our faith in Christ Jesus that we may be justified by faith in Christ and not by observing the law.

Galatians 2:16

$\mathcal{H}$e redeemed us in order that the blessing given to Abraham might come to the Gentiles through Christ Jesus, so that by faith we might receive the promise of the Spirit.

Galatians 3:14

$\mathcal{T}$hose controlled by the sinful nature cannot please God.

Romans 8:8

$\mathcal{T}$he eyes of the LORD range throughout the earth to strengthen those whose hearts are fully committed to him.

2 Chronicles 16:9

$\mathcal{T}$he prayer offered in faith will make the sick person well; the Lord will raise him up.

James 5:15

$\mathcal{T}$he LORD himself goes before you and will be with you; he will never leave you nor forsake you. Do not be afraid; do not be discouraged.

Deuteronomy 31:8

How great is your goodness, which you have
stored up for those who fear you.

Psalm 31:19

Take up the shield of faith, with which you can
extinguish all the flaming arrows of the evil one.

Ephesians 6:16

Let us draw near to God with a sincere heart in
full assurance of faith.

Hebrews 10:22

I say to you: Ask and it will be given to you; seek and you will find; knock and the door will be opened to you. For everyone who asks receives; he who seeks finds; and to him who knocks, the door will be opened.

Luke 11:9–10

*F*ight the good fight, holding on to faith and a good conscience. Some have rejected these and so have shipwrecked their faith.

1 Timothy 1:18–19

*A*s for you, be strong and do not give up, for your work will be rewarded.

2 Chronicles 15:7

The salvation of the righteous comes from the LORD; he is their stronghold in time of trouble. The LORD helps them and delivers them; he delivers them from the wicked and saves them, because they take refuge in him.

Psalm 37:39–40

Cast your cares on the LORD and he will sustain you; he will never let the righteous fall.

Psalm 55:22

You who fear him, trust in the LORD—he is their help and shield.

Psalm 115:11

𝒯he LORD will be your confidence and will keep your foot from being snared.

Proverbs 3:26

𝒯rust in him at all times, O people; pour out your hearts to him, for God is our refuge.

Psalm 62:8

𝒫ut your hope in the LORD, for with the LORD is unfailing love and with him is full redemption.

Psalm 130:7

Have I not commanded you? Be strong and courageous. Do not be terrified; do not be discouraged, for the LORD your God will be with you wherever you go.

Joshua 1:9

The LORD will be a refuge for his people, a stronghold for the people.

Joel 3:16

The LORD your God is with you, he is mighty to save. He will take great delight in you, he will quiet you with his love, he will rejoice over you with singing.

Zephaniah 3:17

Consider how the lilies grow. They do not labor or spin. Yet I tell you, not even Solomon in all his splendor was dressed like one of these. If that is how God clothes the grass of the field, which is here today, and tomorrow is thrown into the fire, how much more will he clothe you, O you of little faith!

Luke 12:27–28

WHAT FAITH CAN DO

$\mathcal{J}$esus said: "I tell you the truth, if you have faith as small as a mustard seed, you can say to this mountain, 'Move from here to there' and it will move. Nothing will be impossible for you."

Matthew 17:20

$\mathcal{J}$esus replied, "I tell you the truth, if you have faith and do not doubt, not only can you do what was done to the fig tree, but also you can say to this mountain, 'Go, throw yourself into the sea,' and it will be done. If you believe, you will receive whatever you ask for in prayer."

Matthew 21:21–22

$\mathscr{H}$e replied, "If you have faith as small as a mustard seed, you can say to this mulberry tree, 'Be uprooted and planted in the sea,' and it will obey you."

Luke 17:6

"Have faith in God," Jesus answered. "I tell you the truth, if anyone says to this mountain, 'Go, throw yourself into the sea,' and does not doubt in his heart but believes that what he says will happen, it will be done for him. Therefore I tell you, whatever you ask for in prayer, believe that you have received it, and it will be yours."

Mark 11:22–24

In the gospel a righteousness from God is revealed, a righteousness that is by faith from first to last, just as it is written: "The righteous will live by faith."

Romans 1:17

Surely this is our God; we trusted in him, and he saved us. This is the LORD, we trusted in him; let us rejoice and be glad in his salvation.

Isaiah 25:9

I tell you the truth, whoever hears my word and believes him who sent me has eternal life and will not be condemned; he has crossed over from death to life.

John 5:24

Everything is possible for him who believes.
Mark 9:23

❧

Jesus replied, "What is impossible with men is possible with God."
Luke 18:27

❧

Nothing is impossible with God.
Luke 1:37

❧

You know that the testing of your faith develops perseverance.
James 1:3

$\mathcal{W}$e also have had the gospel preached to us, just as they did; but the message they heard was of no value to them, because those who heard did not combine it with faith.

Hebrews 4:2

$\mathcal{A}$bram believed the LORD, and he credited it to him as righteousness.

Genesis 15:6

$\mathcal{B}$y faith Moses, when he had grown up, refused to be known as the son of Pharaoh's daughter. He chose to be mistreated along with the people of God rather than to enjoy the pleasures of sin for a short time.

Hebrews 11:24–25

*I*f any of you lacks wisdom, he should ask God,
who gives generously to all without finding fault,
and it will be given to him. But when he asks, he
must believe and not doubt, because he who doubts
is like a wave of the sea, blown and
tossed by the wind.

James 1:5–6

*I*t is written: "I believed; therefore I have spoken."
With that same spirit of faith we also believe and
therefore speak.

2 Corinthians 4:13

Fear not, for I have redeemed you; I have summoned you by name; you are mine. When you pass through the waters, I will be with you; and when you pass through the rivers, they will not sweep over you. When you walk through the fire, you will not be burned; the flames will not set you ablaze. For I am the LORD, your God, the Holy One of Israel, your Savior.

Isaiah 43:1–3

I, even I, am the LORD, and apart from me there is no savior.

Isaiah 43:11

*W*hat more shall I say? I do not have time to tell about Gideon, Barak, Samson, Jephthah, David, Samuel and the prophets, who through faith conquered kingdoms, administered justice, and gained what was promised; who shut the mouths of lions, quenched the fury of the flames, and escaped the edge of the sword; whose weakness was turned to strength; and who became powerful in battle and routed foreign armies.

Hebrews 11:32–34

*N*othing can hinder the L ORD from saving, whether by many or by few.

1 Samuel 14:6

$\mathcal{W}$e constantly pray for you, that our God may count you worthy of his calling, and that by his power he may fulfill every good purpose of yours and every act prompted by your faith.

2 Thessalonians 1:1

$\mathcal{C}$onsequently, faith comes from hearing the message, and the message is heard through the word of Christ.

Romans 10:17

$\mathcal{A}$ccording to your faith will it be done to you.

Matthew 9:29

For this very reason, make every effort to add to your faith goodness; and to goodness, knowledge; and to knowledge, self-control; and to self-control, perseverance; and to perseverance, godliness; and to godliness, brotherly kindness; and to brotherly kindness, love. For if you possess these qualities in increasing measure, they will keep you from being ineffective and unproductive in your knowledge of our Lord Jesus Christ.

2 Peter 1:5–8

I have set the LORD always before me. Because he is at my right hand, I will not be shaken.

Psalm 16:8

Let us fix our eyes on Jesus, the author and perfecter of our faith, who for the joy set before him endured the cross, scorning its shame, and sat down at the right hand of the throne of God.

Hebrews 12:2

Do not think of yourself more highly than you ought, but rather think of yourself with sober judgment, in accordance with the measure of faith God has given you.

Romans 12:3

You, O Lord, keep my lamp burning; my God turns my darkness into light. With your help I can advance against a troop; with my God I can scale a wall.

Psalm 18:28–29

*W*e also thank God continually because, when you received the word of God, which you heard from us, you accepted it not as the word of men, but as it actually is, the word of God, which is at work in you who believe.

1 Thessalonians 2:13

*B*y faith we eagerly await through the Spirit the righteousness for which we hope. For in Christ Jesus neither circumcision nor uncircumcision has any value. The only thing that counts is faith expressing itself through love.

Galatians 5:5–6

$\mathcal{D}$o not worry about your life, what you will eat; or about your body, what you will wear. Life is more than food, and the body more than clothes. Consider the ravens: They do not sow or reap, they have no storeroom or barn; yet God feeds them. And how much more valuable you are than birds!

Luke 12:22–24

EVEN IF OUR
FAITH IS SMALL

And why do you worry about clothes? See how the lilies of the field grow. They do not labor or spin. Yet I tell you that not even Solomon in all his splendor was dressed like one of these. If that is how God clothes the grass of the field, which is here today and tomorrow is thrown into the fire, will he not much more clothe you, O you of little faith? So do not worry.

Matthew 6:28–31

Jesus said, "Did I not tell you that if you believed, you would see the glory of God?"

John 11:40

I tell you the truth, anyone who has faith in me will do what I have been doing. He will do even greater things than these, because I am going to the Father.

John 14:12

The Scripture says, "Anyone who trusts in him will never be put to shame."

Romans 10:11

In Scripture it says: "See, I lay a stone in Zion, a chosen and precious cornerstone, and the one who trusts in him will never be put to shame."

1 Peter 2:6

He got into the boat and his disciples followed him. Without warning, a furious storm came up on the lake, so that the waves swept over the boat. But Jesus was sleeping. The disciples went and woke him, saying, "Lord, save us! We're going to drown!" He replied, "You of little faith, why are you so afraid?" Then he got up and rebuked the winds and the waves, and it was completely calm.

Matthew 8:23–26

Jesus said: "If you have faith as small as a mustard seed, you can say to this mountain, 'Move from here to there' and it will move. Nothing will be impossible for you."

Matthew 17:20

$\mathcal{J}$esus went out to them, walking on the lake. When the disciples saw him walking on the lake, they were terrified. But Jesus immediately said to them: "Take courage! It is I. Don't be afraid." "Lord, if it's you," Peter replied, "tell me to come to you on the water." "Come," he said. Then Peter got down out of the boat, walked on the water and came toward Jesus. But when he saw the wind, he was afraid and, beginning to sink, cried out, "Lord, save me!" Immediately Jesus reached out his hand and caught him. "You of little faith," he said, "why did you doubt?" And when they climbed into the boat, the wind died down.

Matthew 14:25–32

*H*e has reconciled you by Christ's physical body through death to present you holy in his sight, without blemish and free from accusation—if you continue in your faith, established and firm, not moved from the hope held out in the gospel.

Colossians 1:22–23

*S*ee to it … that none of you has a sinful, unbelieving heart that turns away from the living God.

Hebrews 3:12

I will leave within you the meek and humble, who trust in the name of the LORD.

Zephaniah 3:12

𝓘 do believe; help me overcome my unbelief!
Mark 9:24

𝓗is disciples were in the house again, and
Thomas was with them. Though the doors were
locked, Jesus came and stood among them and said,
"Peace be with you!" Then he said to Thomas, "Put
your finger here; see my hands. Reach out your
hand and put it into my side. Stop doubting and
believe." Thomas said to him, "My Lord and my
God!" Then Jesus told him, "Because you have seen
me, you have believed; blessed are those who have
not seen and yet have believed."
John 20:26–29

$\mathcal{D}$o not set you heart on what you will eat or drink; do not worry about it. For the pagan world runs after all such things, and your Father knows that you need them. But seek his kingdom and these things will be given to you as well. Do not be afraid, little flock, for your Father has been pleased to give you the kingdom.

Luke 12:29–32

How We Can Build Our Faith

*T*hough I am absent from you in body, I am present with you in spirit and delight to see how orderly you are and how firm your faith in Christ is. So then, just as you received Christ Jesus as Lord, continue to live in him, rooted and built up in him, strengthened in the faith as you were taught, and overflowing with thankfulness.

Colossians 2:5–7

*A*nd the God of all grace, who called you to his eternal glory in Christ, after you have suffered a little while, will himself restore you and make you strong, firm and steadfast.

1 Peter 5:10

May our Lord Jesus Christ himself and God our Father, who loved us and by his grace gave us eternal encouragement and good hope, encourage your hearts and strengthen you in every good deed and word.

2 Thessalonians 2:16–17

Therefore, dear friends, since you already know this, be on your guard so that you may not be carried away by the error of lawless men and fall from your secure position. But grow in the grace and knowledge of our Lord and Savior Jesus Christ. To him be glory both now and forever! Amen.

2 Peter 3:17–18

*H*e has reconciled you by Christ's physical body through death to present you holy in his sight, without blemish and free from accusation—if you continue in your faith, established and firm, not moved from the hope held out in the gospel. This is the gospel that you heard.

Colossians 1:22–23

*S*peaking the truth in love, we will in all things grow up into him who is the Head, that is, Christ. From him the whole body, joined and held together by every supporting ligament, grows and builds itself up in love, as each part does its work.

Ephesians 4:15–16

$\mathcal{I}$ pray that out of his glorious riches he may strengthen you with power through his Spirit in your inner being, so that Christ may dwell in your hearts through faith.

Ephesians 3:16–17

$\mathcal{E}$veryone who hears these words of mine and puts them into practice is like a wise man who built his house on the rock. The rain came down, the streams rose, and the winds blew and beat against that house; yet it did not fall, because it had its foundation on the rock.

Matthew 7:24–25

$\mathscr{S}$tand firm. Let nothing move you. Always give yourselves fully to the work of the Lord, because you know that your labor in the Lord is not in vain.

1 Corinthians 15:58

$\mathscr{N}$ow to him who is able to establish you by my gospel and the proclamation of Jesus Christ, according to the revelation of the mystery hidden for long ages past, but now revealed and made known through the prophetic writings by the command of the eternal God, so that all nations might believe and obey him—to the only wise God be glory forever through Jesus Christ! Amen.

Romans 16:25–27

Faith in the
Tough Times
of Life

Though he slay me, yet will I hope in him; I will surely defend my ways to his face.

Job 13:15

Consider it pure joy, my brothers, whenever you face trials of many kinds, because you know that the testing of your faith develops perseverance. Perseverance must finish its work so that you may be mature and complete, not lacking anything.

James 1:2–4

*H*e knows the way that I take; when he has tested
me, I will come forth as gold.

Job 23:10

❧

*D*o not be afraid, for I am with you.

Isaiah 43:5

Moses answered the people, "Do not be afraid. Stand firm and you will see the deliverance the LORD will bring you today."

Exodus 14:13

For the LORD watches over the way of the righteous, but the way of the wicked will perish.

Psalm 1:6

I will refine them like silver and test them like gold. They will call on my name and I will answer them; I will say, "They are my people," and they will say, "The LORD is our God."

Zechariah 13:9

*Y*ou may have had to suffer grief in all kinds of trials. These have come so that your faith—of greater worth than gold, which perishes even though refined by fire—may be proved genuine and may result in praise, glory and honor when Jesus Christ is revealed.

1 Peter 1:6–7

*N*o one will be able to stand up against you all the days of your life. As I was with Moses, so I will be with you; I will never leave you nor forsake you.

Joshua 1:5

It has been granted to you on behalf of Christ not only to believe on him, but also to suffer for him.

Philippians 1:29

If we are children, then we are heirs—heirs of God and co–heirs with Christ, if indeed we share in his sufferings in order that we may also share in his glory. I consider that our present sufferings are not worth comparing with the glory that will be revealed in us.

Romans 8:17–18

When the Son of Man comes, will he find faith on the earth?

Luke 18:8

*H*e said to me, "My grace is sufficient for you, for my power is made perfect in weakness." Therefore I will boast all the more gladly about my weaknesses, so that Christ's power may rest on me.

2 Corinthians 12:9

*T*he God of all grace, who called you to his eternal glory in Christ, after you have suffered a little while, will himself restore you and make you strong, firm and steadfast.

1 Peter 5:10

*T*rust in him at all times, O people; pour out your hearts to him, for God is our refuge.

Psalm 62:8

Commit your way to the LORD; trust in him and he will do this: He will make your righteousness shine like the dawn ... Be still before the LORD and wait patiently for him; do not fret when men succeed in their ways, when they carry out their wicked schemes.

Psalm 37:5–7

This is what the LORD says to you: "Do not be afraid or discouraged because of this vast army. For the battle is not yours, but God's."

2 Chronicles 20:15

The LORD your God is testing you to find out whether you love him with all your heart and with all your soul. It is the LORD your God you must follow, and him you must revere. Keep his commands and obey him; serve him and hold fast to him.

Deuteronomy 13:3–4

You will not have to fight this battle. Take up your positions; stand firm and see the deliverance the LORD will give you … Do not be afraid; do not be discouraged.

2 Chronicles 20:17

Even though I walk through the valley of the shadow of death, I will fear no evil, for you are with me; your rod and your staff, they comfort me.

Psalm 23:4

Do not tremble, do not be afraid. Did I not proclaim this and foretell it long ago? You are my witnesses. Is there any God besides me? No, there is no other Rock; I know not one.

Isaiah 44:8

Cast your cares on the LORD and he will sustain you; he will never let the righteous fall.

Psalm 55:22

I am convinced that neither death nor life, neither angels nor demons, neither the present nor the future, nor any powers, neither height nor depth, nor anything else in all creation, will be able to separate us from the love of God that is in Christ Jesus.

Romans 8:38–39

If I rise on the wings of the dawn, if I settle on the far side of the sea, even there your hand will guide me, your right hand will hold me fast.

Psalm 139:9–10

Jesus said: "I have told you these things, so that in me you may have peace. In this world you will have trouble. But take heart! I have overcome the world."

John 16:33

Fear not, for I have redeemed you; I have summoned you by name; you are mine. When you pass through the waters, I will be with you; and when you pass through the rivers, they will not sweep over you. When you walk through the fire, you will not be burned; the flames will not set you ablaze. For I am the LORD, your God.

Isaiah 43:1–3

Though the fig tree does not bud and there are no grapes on the vines, though the olive crop fails and the fields produce no food, though there are no sheep in the pen and no cattle in the stalls, yet I will rejoice in the LORD, I will be joyful in God my Savior. The Sovereign LORD is my strength; he makes my feet like the feet of a deer, he enables me to go on the heights.

Habakkuk 3:17–18

❧

I watch in hope for the LORD, I wait for God my Savior; my God will hear me.

Micah 7:7

Against all hope, Abraham in hope believed and so became the father of many nations, just as it had been said to him, "So shall your offspring be." Without weakening in his faith, he faced the fact that his body was as good as dead—since he was about a hundred years old—and that Sarah's womb was also dead. Yet he did not waver through unbelief regarding the promise of God, but was strengthened in his faith and gave glory to God, being fully persuaded that God had power to do what he had promised. This is why "it was credited to him as righteousness."

Romans 4:18–22

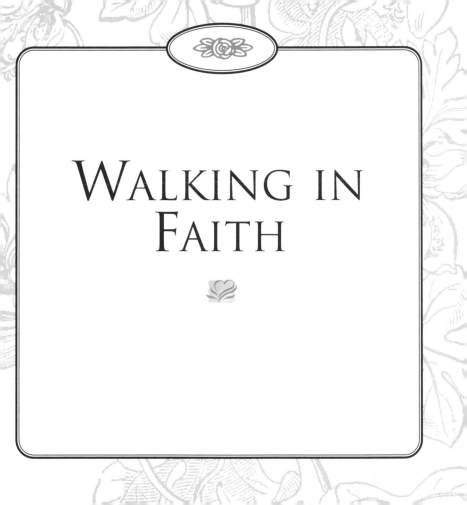

WALKING IN FAITH

*W*hat does the L ORD your God ask of you but to fear the L ORD your God, to walk in all his ways, to love him, to serve the L ORD your God with all your heart and with all your soul.

Deuteronomy 10:12

*W*e live by faith, not by sight.

2 Corinthians 5:7

*W*alk in all the way that the L ORD your God has commanded you, so that you may live and prosper and prolong your days.

Deuteronomy 5:33

If we walk in the light, as he is in the light, we have fellowship with one another, and the blood of Jesus, his Son, purifies us from all sin.

1 John 1:7

We, too, have put our faith in Christ Jesus that we may be justified by faith in Christ.

Galatians 2:16

The life I live in the body, I live by faith in the Son of God, who loved me and gave himself for me.

Galatians 2:20

$\mathcal{B}$e very careful to keep the commandment and the
law that Moses the servant of the Lord gave you: to
love the Lord your God, to walk in all his ways, to obey
his commands, to hold fast to him and to serve him
with all your heart and all your soul.

Joshua 22:5

$\mathcal{B}$lessed are all who fear the Lord, who
walk in his ways.

Psalm 128:1

$\mathcal{M}$ay he turn our hearts to him, to walk in all his ways
and to keep the commands, decrees and regulations he
gave our fathers.

1 Kings 8:58

$\mathcal{I}$ am not ashamed, because I know whom I have believed, and am convinced that he is able to guard what I have entrusted to him for that day.

2 Timothy 1:12

$\mathcal{G}$od is not a man, that he should lie, nor a son of man, that he should change his mind. Does he speak and then not act? Does he promise and not fulfill?

Numbers 23:19

Observe what the LORD your God requires: Walk in his ways, and keep his decrees and commands, his laws and requirements, as written in the Law of Moses, so that you may prosper in all you do and wherever you go.

1 Kings 2:3

Teach me your way, O LORD, and I will walk in your truth; give me an undivided heart, that I may fear your name.

Psalm 86:11

The ways of the LORD are right; the righteous walk in them.

Hosea 14:9

Though I walk in the midst of trouble, you preserve my life; you stretch out your hand against the anger of my foes, with your right hand you save me. The LORD will fulfill [his purpose] for me.

Psalm 138:7–8

Trust in the LORD forever, for the LORD, the LORD, is the Rock eternal.

Isaiah 26:4

Trust in the LORD and do good; dwell in the land and enjoy safe pasture.

Psalm 37:3

$\mathcal{J}$esus said: "I am the light of the world. Whoever
follows me will never walk in darkness, but
will have the light of life."
John 8:12

$\mathcal{C}$learly no one is justified before God by the law,
because, "The righteous will live by faith."
Galatians 3:11

$\mathcal{J}$ can do everything through him who
gives me strength.
Philippians 4:13

You ... like living stones, are being built into a spiritual house to be a holy priesthood, offering spiritual sacrifices acceptable to God through Jesus Christ.

1 Peter 2:5

I am God Almighty; walk before me and be blameless.

Genesis 17:1

Cast your cares on the LORD and he will sustain you; he will never let the righteous fall.

Psalm 55:22

$\mathcal{I}$ strive always to keep my conscience clear
before God and man.

Acts 24:16

$\mathcal{W}$hat does the LORD require of you? To act justly and
to love mercy and to walk humbly with your God.

Micah 6:8

$\mathcal{R}$emember, O LORD, how I have walked before you
faithfully and with wholehearted devotion and have
done what is good in your eyes.

Isaiah 38:3

*Y*ou have declared this day that the LORD is your God and that you will walk in his ways, that you will keep his decrees, commands and laws, and that you will obey him.

Deuteronomy 26:17

*I*f we claim to have fellowship with him yet walk in the darkness, we lie and do not live by the truth.

1 John 1:6

*B*ecause the Sovereign LORD helps me, I will not be disgraced. Therefore have I set my face like flint, and I know I will not be put to shame.

Isaiah 50:7

Trust in the LORD with all your heart and lean not on your own understanding; in all your ways acknowledge him, and he will make your paths straight.

Proverbs 3:5–6

He will teach us his ways, so that we may walk in his paths.

Micah 4:2

I gave them this command: Obey me, and I will be your God and you will be my people. Walk in all the ways I command you, that it may go well with you.

Jeremiah 7:23

$\mathcal{L}$eave your simple ways and you will live; walk in the way of understanding.

Proverbs 9:6

$\mathcal{L}$et your eyes look straight ahead, fix your gaze directly before you. Make level paths for your feet and take only ways that are firm. Do not swerve to the right or the left; keep your foot from evil.

Proverbs 4:25–27

$\mathcal{K}$eep the way of the LORD and walk in it.

Judges 2:22

$\mathcal{B}$e careful to do what the LORD your God has commanded you; do not turn aside to the right or to the left.

Deuteronomy 5:32

$\mathcal{I}$t is the LORD your God you must follow, and him you must revere. Keep his commands and obey him; serve him and hold fast to him.

Deuteronomy 13:4

$\mathcal{B}$lessed are those who have learned to acclaim you, who walk in the light of your presence, O LORD.

Psalm 89:15

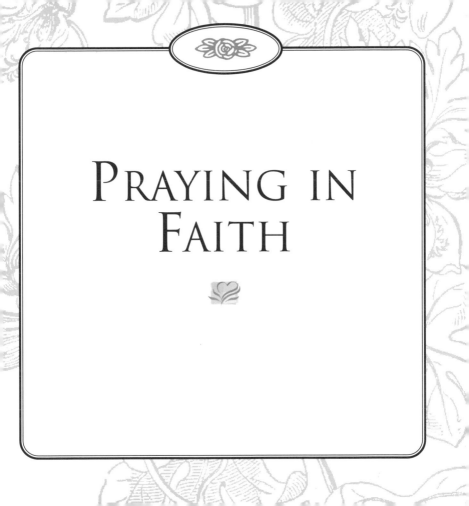

PRAYING IN FAITH

Hear, O LORD, my righteous plea; listen to my cry.
Give ear to my prayer—it does not
rise from deceitful lips.

Psalm 17:1

The LORD detests the sacrifice of the wicked, but the
prayer of the upright pleases him.

Proverbs 15:8

For the eyes of the Lord are on the righteous and his
ears are attentive to their prayer, but the face of the
Lord is against those who do evil.

1 Peter 3:12

Is any one of you sick? He should call the elders of the church to pray over him and anoint him with oil in the name of the Lord. And the prayer offered in faith will make the sick person well; the Lord will raise him up. If he has sinned, he will be forgiven. Therefore confess your sins to each other and pray for each other so that you may be healed.

James 5:14–16

We know that God does not listen to sinners. He listens to the godly.

John 9:31

$\mathcal{J}$esus said: "I tell you the truth, if anyone says to this mountain, 'Go, throw yourself into the sea,' and does not doubt in his heart but believes that what he says will happen, it will be done for him. Therefore I tell you, whatever you ask for in prayer, believe that you have received it, and it will be yours."

Mark 11:23–24

$\mathcal{J}$f I had cherished sin in my heart, the Lord would not have listened; but God has surely listened and heard my voice in prayer.

Psalm 66:18–19

The LORD is near to all who call on him, to all who call on him in truth.

Psalm 145:18

The righteous cry out, and the LORD hears them; he delivers them from all their troubles.

Psalm 34:17

If any of you lacks wisdom, he should ask God, who gives generously to all without finding fault, and it will be given to him. But when he asks, he must believe and not doubt, because he who doubts is like a wave of the sea, blown and tossed by the wind.

James 1:5–6

Jesus said: "You have so little faith. I tell you the truth, if you have faith as small as a mustard seed, you can say to this mountain, 'Move from here to there' and it will move. Nothing will be impossible for you."

Matthew 17:20

The LORD said: "My eyes will be open and my ears attentive to the prayers offered in this place."

2 Chronicles 7:15

You will call, and the LORD will answer; you will cry for help, and he will say: Here am I.

Isaiah 58:9

*T*hose who know your name will trust in you, for you, LORD, have never forsaken those who seek you.

Psalm 9:10

*T*he Spirit helps us in our weakness. We do not know what we ought to pray for, but the Spirit himself intercedes for us with groans that words cannot express. And he who searches our hearts knows the mind of the Spirit, because the Spirit intercedes for the saints in accordance with God's will.

Romans 8:26–27

*S*ome trust in chariots and some in horses, but we trust in the name of the LORD our God.

Psalm 20:7

The LORD is my rock, my fortress and my deliverer; my God is my rock, in whom I take refuge. He is my shield and the horn of my salvation, my stronghold. I call to the LORD, who is worthy of praise, and I am saved from my enemies.

Psalm 18:2–3

This is what the LORD says to you: "Do not be afraid or discouraged. Stand firm and see the deliverance the LORD will give you."

2 Chronicles 20:15, 17

Let all who take refuge in you be glad; let them ever sing for joy. Spread your protection over them, that those who love your name may rejoice in you. For surely, O LORD, you bless the righteous: you surround them with your favor as with a shield.

Psalm 5:11–12

SOME WHO PRAYED IN FAITH AND SAW GOD ANSWER

"$\mathcal{D}$o not be afraid or discouraged because of the king of Assyria and the vast army with him, for there is a greater power with us than with him. With him is only the arm of flesh, but with us is the Lord our God to help us and to fight our battles." And the people gained confidence from what Hezekiah the king of Judah said.

2 Chronicles 32:7–8

$\mathcal{T}$wo blind men followed [Jesus], calling out, "Have mercy on us, Son of David!" … He asked them, "Do you believe that I am able to do this?" "Yes, Lord," they replied. Then he touched their eyes and said, "According to your faith will it be done to you."

Matthew 9:27–29

$\mathcal{A}$ man with leprosy came and knelt before him and said, "Lord, if you are willing, you can make me clean." Jesus reached out his hand and touched the man. "I am willing," he said. "Be clean!" Immediately he was cured of his leprosy.

Matthew 8:2–3

$\mathcal{A}$ woman who had been subject to bleeding for twelve years came up behind him and touched the edge of his cloak. She said to herself, "If I only touch his cloak, I will be healed." Jesus turned and saw her. "Take heart, daughter," he said, "your faith has healed you." And the woman was healed from that moment.

Matthew 9:20–22

I trust in your unfailing love; my heart rejoices in
your salvation. I will sing to the LORD,
for he has been good to me.

Psalm 13:5–6

*S*ome men came carrying a paralytic on a mat and
tried to take him into the house to lay him before Jesus.
When they could not find a way to do this because of
the crowd, they went up on the roof and lowered him
on his mat through the tiles into the middle of the
crowd, right in front of Jesus. When Jesus saw their
faith, he said, "Friend, your sins are forgiven."

Luke 5:18–20

The king of Jericho sent this message to Rahab: "Bring out the men who came to you and entered your house, because they have come to spy out the whole land."

But the woman had taken the two men and hidden them. She said, "Yes, the men came to me, but I did not know where they had come from. At dusk, when it was time to close the city gate, the men left. I don't know which way they went. Go after them quickly. You may catch up with them." … As soon as the pursuers had gone out, the gate was shut.

Before the spies lay down for the night, she went up on the roof and said to them, "I know that the LORD has given this land to you … Now then, please swear to me by the LORD that you will show kindness to my family, because I have shown kindness to you. Give me a sure sign that you will spare the lives of my father and mother, my brothers and sisters, and all who belong to them, and that you will save us from death."

"Our lives for your lives!" the men assured her.

The men said to her, "This oath you made us swear will not be binding on us unless, when we enter the land, you have tied this scarlet cord in the window through which you let us down, and unless you have brought your father and mother, your brothers and all your family into your house. ... But if you tell what we are doing, we will be released from the oath you made us swear."

"Agreed," she replied. "Let it be as you say."

So she sent them away and they departed. And
she tied the scarlet cord
in the window.

[So] Joshua spared Rahab the prostitute, with her
family and all who belonged to her, because she hid
the men Joshua had sent as spies to Jericho—and
she lives among the Israelites to this day.

Joshua 2:3–9,12–14,17–21; 6:25

When Jesus had entered Capernaum, a centurion came to him, asking for help. "Lord," he said, "my servant lies at home paralyzed and in terrible suffering." Jesus said to him, "I will go and heal him." The centurion replied, "Lord, I do not deserve to have you come under my roof. But just say the word, and my servant will be healed.

For I myself am a man under authority, with soldiers under me. I tell this one, 'Go,' and he goes; and that one, 'Come,' and he comes. I say to my servant, 'Do this,' and he does it."

*W*hen Jesus heard this, he was astonished and said to those following him, "I tell you the truth, I have not found anyone in Israel with such great faith ..." Then Jesus said to the centurion, "Go! It will be done just as you believed it would." And his servant was healed at that very hour.

Matthew 8:10–13

[When a certain royal official] heard that Jesus had arrived in Galilee from Judea, he went to him and begged him to come and heal his son, who was close to death. The royal official said, "Sir, come down before my child dies."

Jesus replied, "You may go. Your son will live." The man took Jesus at his word and departed. While he was still on the way, his servants met him with the news that his boy was living. When he inquired as to the time when his son got better … the father realized that this was the exact time at which Jesus had said to him, "Your son will live." So he and all his household believed.

John 4:46–53

In bitterness of soul Hannah wept much and prayed to the LORD. And she made a vow, saying, "O LORD Almighty, if you will only look upon your servant's misery and remember me, and not forget your servant but give her a son, then I will give him to the LORD for all the days of his life, and no razor will ever be used on his head."

As she kept on praying to the LORD, Eli observed her mouth. Hannah was praying in her heart, and her lips were moving but her voice was not heard. Eli thought she was drunk …

Hannah replied, "I am a woman who is deeply troubled. I have not been drinking wine or beer; I was pouring out my soul to the LORD. Do not take your servant for a wicked woman; I have been praying here out of my great anguish and grief."

Eli answered, "Go in peace, and may the God of Israel grant you what you have asked of him."
She said, "May your servant find favor in your eyes." Then she went her way and ate something, and her face was no longer downcast.

Elkanah lay with Hannah his wife, and the LORD remembered her. So in the course of time Hannah conceived and gave birth to a son.
She named him Samuel.

They brought the boy to Eli, and she said to him, "As surely as you live, my lord, I am the woman who stood here beside you praying to the LORD. I prayed for this child, and the LORD has granted me what I asked of him. So now I give him to the LORD. For his whole life

he will be given over to the Lord." And he
worshiped the Lord there.

1 Samuel 1:10–20,25–28

*A*gainst all hope, Abraham in hope believed and
so became the father of many nations, just as it had
been said to him, "So shall your offspring be."
Without weakening in his faith, he faced the fact
that his body was as good as dead—since he was
about a hundred years old—and that Sarah's womb
was also dead. Yet he did not waver through
unbelief regarding the promise of God, but was
strengthened in his faith and gave glory to God,
being fully persuaded that God had power to do
what he had promised.

Romans 4:18–21

The commander of [Jabin's] army was Sisera, who lived in Harosheth Haggoyim. Because he had nine hundred iron chariots and had cruelly oppressed the Israelites for twenty years, they cried to the LORD for help.

Deborah, a prophetess, the wife of Lappidoth, was leading Israel at that time ... She sent for Barak son of Abinoam ... and said to him, "The LORD, the God of Israel, commands you: 'Go, take with you ten thousand men of Naphtali and Zebulun and lead the way to Mount Tabor. I will lure Sisera, the commander of Jabin's army, with his chariots and his troops to the Kishon River and give him into your hands.'"

Barak said to her, "If you go with me, I will go; but if you don't go with me, I won't go."
"Very well," Deborah said, "I will go with you. But because of the way you are going about this, the honor will not be yours, for the LORD will hand Sisera over to a woman." So

Deborah went with Barak to Kedesh, where he summoned Zebulun and Naphtali. Ten thousand men followed him, and Deborah also went with him. Sisera gathered together his nine hundred iron chariots and all the men with him.

Then Deborah said to Barak, "Go! This is the day the LORD has given Sisera into your hands. Has not the LORD gone ahead of you?" So Barak went down Mount Tabor, followed by ten thousand men. At Barak's advance, the LORD routed Sisera and all his chariots and army by the sword, and Sisera abandoned his chariot and fled on foot. But Barak pursued the chariots and army as far as Harosheth Haggoyim. All the troops of Sisera fell by the sword; not a man was left.

Judges 4:2–10,13–16

[Haman, one of the king's nobles] said to King Xerxes, "There is a certain people dispersed and scattered among the peoples in all the provinces of your kingdom whose customs are different from those of all other people and who do not obey the king's laws; it is not in the king's best interest to tolerate them. If it pleases the king, let a decree be issued to destroy them.

The king said to Haman, "Do with the people as you please."
[Mordecai urged Esther] to go into the king's presence to beg for mercy and plead with him for her people.

"Do not think that because you are in the king's house you alone of all the Jews will escape. For if you remain silent at this time, relief and deliverance for the Jews will arise from another place, but you and your father's family will perish. And who knows but that you have come to royal position for such a time as this?"

[Esther replied]: "Go, gather together all the Jews who are in Susa, and fast for me. Do not eat or drink for three days, night or day. I and my maids will fast as you do. When this is done, I will go to the king, even though it is against the law.
And if I perish, I perish."

On the third day Esther put on her royal robes and stood in the inner court of the palace, in front of the king's hall.
The king asked, "What is it, Queen Esther? What is your request? Even up to half the kingdom, it will be given you."

"If it pleases the king," replied Esther, "let the king, together with Haman, come today to a banquet I have prepared for him."

"*B*ring Haman at once," the king said, "so that we may do what Esther asks." So the king and Haman went to the banquet Esther had prepared.

The king again asked Esther, "Now what is your petition? It will be given you.

*W*hat is your request? Even up to half the kingdom, it will be granted."

Esther replied, "My petition and my request is this: ... Let the king and Haman come tomorrow to the banquet I will prepare for them.

Then I will answer the king's question."

*S*o the king and Haman went to dine with Queen Esther, and as they were drinking wine on that second day, the king again asked, "Queen Esther, what is your petition? It will be given you. What is your request? Even up to half the kingdom, it will be granted."

Then Queen Esther answered, "If I have found favor with you, O king, and if it pleases your majesty, grant me my life—this is my petition. And spare my people—this is my request."

King Xerxes asked Queen Esther, "Who is he? Where is the man who has dared to do such a thing?" Esther said, "The adversary and enemy is this vile Haman." Then Haman was terrified before the king and queen.

So they hanged Haman on the gallows he had prepared for Mordecai. Then the king's fury subsided.
The enemies of the Jews had hoped to overpower them, but now the tables were turned and the Jews got the upper hand over those who hated them.

Esther 3:8–10; 4:8,13–16; 5:1,3–7; 7:1–3,5–6,10; 9:1

Three times a day [Daniel] got down on his knees and prayed, giving thanks to his God, just as he had done before. Then [some] men went as a group and found Daniel praying and asking God for help.

So they went to the king and spoke to him about his royal decree … They said to the king, "Daniel, who is one of the exiles from Judah, pays no attention to you O king, or to the decree you put in writing. He still prays three times a day."

When the king heard this, he was greatly distressed; he was determined to rescue Daniel and made every effort until sundown to save him.

The men went as a group to the king and said to him, "Remember, O king, that according to the law of the Medes and Persians no decree or edict that the king issues can be changed."

So the king gave the order, and they brought Daniel and threw him into the lions' den. The king said to Daniel, "May your God, whom you serve continually, rescue you!"

A stone was brought and placed over the mouth of the den, and the king sealed it with his own signet ring and with the rings of his nobles, so that Daniel's situation might not be changed. Then the king returned to his palace and spent the night without eating and without any entertainment being brought to him. And he could not sleep.

At the first light of dawn, the king got up and hurried to the lions' den. When he came near the den, he called to Daniel in an anguished voice, "Daniel, servant of the living God, has your God, whom you serve continually, been able to rescue you from the lions?"

Daniel answered, "O king, live forever! My God sent his angel, and he shut the mouths of the lions. They have not hurt me, because I was found innocent in his sight. Nor have I ever done any wrong before you, O king."

The king was overjoyed and gave orders to lift Daniel out of the den. And when Daniel was lifted from the den, no wound was found on him, because he had trusted in his God.

Daniel 6:10–23

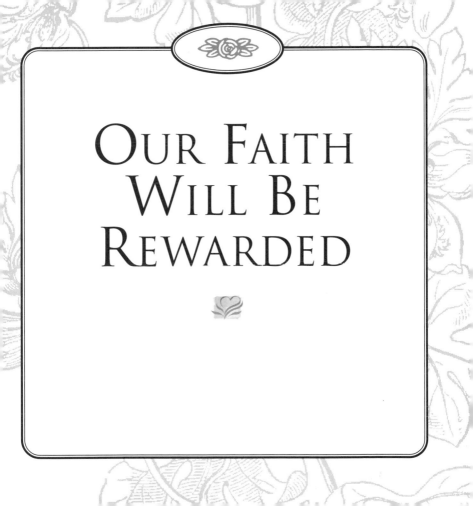

Our Faith
Will Be
Rewarded

*Y*ou will keep in perfect peace him whose mind is steadfast, because he trusts in you. Trust in the L ORD forever, for the L ORD, the L ORD, is the Rock eternal.

Isaiah 26:3–4

*B*lessed is the [one] who trusts in the L ORD, whose confidence is in him. He will be like a tree planted by the water that sends out its roots by the stream. It does not fear when heat comes; its leaves are always green. It has no worries in a year of drought and never fails to bear fruit.

Jeremiah 17:7–8

The LORD longs to be gracious to you; he rises to show you compassion. For the LORD is a God of justice. Blessed are all who wait for him!

Isaiah 30:18

Whoever gives heed to instruction prospers, and blessed is [the one] who trusts in the LORD.

Proverbs 16:20

I have told you these things, so that in me you may have peace. In this world you will have trouble. But take heart! I have overcome the world.

John 16:33

May the God of hope fill you with all joy and peace as you trust in him, so that you may overflow with hope by the power of the Holy Spirit.

Romans 15:13

Trust in him at all times, O people; pour out your hearts to him, for God is our refuge.

Psalm 62:8

The LORD is good, a refuge in times of trouble. He cares for those who trust in him.

Nahum 1:7

*B*lessed are those whose strength is in you, who have set their hearts on pilgrimage. They go from strength to strength, till each appears before God in Zion.

Psalm 84:5,7

I will build them up and not tear them down; I will plant them and not uproot them. I will give them a heart to know me, that I am the LORD. They will be my people, and I will be their God.

Jeremiah 24:6–7

Keep your lives free from the love of money and be content with what you have, because God has said, "Never will I leave you; never will I forsake you." So we say with confidence, "The Lord is my helper; I will not be afraid. What can man do to me?"

Hebrews 13:5–6

Let all who take refuge in you be glad; let them ever sing for joy. Spread your protection over them, that those who love your name may rejoice in you. For surely, O LORD, you bless the righteous; you surround them with your favor as with a shield.

Psalm 5:11–12

It is God who arms me with strength and makes my way perfect. He makes my feet like the feet of a deer; he enables me to stand on the heights.

2 Samuel 22:33–34

The eyes of the LORD are on those who fear him, on those whose hope is in his unfailing love.

Psalm 33:18

Be faithful, even to the point of death, and I will give you the crown of life.

Revelation 2:10

The ransomed of the LORD will return. They will enter Zion with singing; everlasting joy will crown their heads. Gladness and joy will overtake them, and sorrow and sighing will flee away.

Isaiah 35:10

Has not God chosen those who are poor in the eyes of the world to be rich in faith and to inherit the kingdom he promised those who love him?

James 2:5

Therefore I tell you, whatever you ask for in prayer, believe that you have received it, and it will be yours.

Mark 11:24

If you belong to Christ, then you are Abraham's seed, and heirs according to the promise.

Galatians 3:29

Everyone who has left houses or brothers or sisters or father or mother or children or fields for my sake will receive a hundred times as much and will inherit eternal life.

Matthew 19:29

All men will hate you because of me, but he who stands firm to the end will be saved.

Matthew 10:22

$\mathcal{D}$o not be afraid. Stand firm and you will see the deliverance the LORD will bring you today.

Exodus 14:13

$\mathcal{T}$he LORD himself goes before you and will be with you; he will never leave you nor forsake you. Do not be afraid; do not be discouraged.

Deuteronomy 31:8

$\mathcal{H}$ave I not commanded you? Be strong and courageous. Do not be terrified; do not be discouraged, for the LORD your God will be with you wherever you go.

Joshua 1:9

$\mathcal{B}$e strong and do not give up, for your work
will be rewarded.

2 Chronicles 15:7

$\mathcal{S}$trengthen the feeble hands, steady the knees that
give way; say to those with fearful hearts, "Be strong,
do not fear; your God will come."

Isaiah 35:3–4

$\mathcal{T}$he salvation of the righteous comes from the
LORD; he is their stronghold in time of trouble. The
LORD helps them and delivers them; he delivers
them from the wicked and saves them, because they
take refuge in him.

Psalm 37:39–40

How great is your goodness, which you have stored
up for those who fear you.

Psalm 31:19

Cast your cares on the LORD and he will sustain you;
he will never let the righteous fall.

Psalm 55:22

The LORD will be your confidence and will keep your
foot from being snared.

Proverbs 3:26

Put your hope in the LORD, for with the LORD is
unfailing love and with him is full redemption.

Psalm 130:7